Learn WordPerfect in a Day

Felicia Case

Wordware Publishing, Inc.

Library of Congress Cataloging-in-Publication Data

Case, Felicia
   Learn WordPerfect in a day
   p.   cm.
   Includes index.
   ISBN 1-55622-189-4
   1. WordPerfect (Computer program). 2. Word processing. I. Title.
Z52.5.W65C37 1990
652.5'536—dc20   90-12629
                                           CIP

ISBN 1-55622-189-4
10 9 8 7 6 5 4 3
9007

WordPerfect is a registered trademark of WordPerfect Corporation.

All inquiries for volume purchases of this book should be addressed to Wordware
Publishing, Inc., at the above address. Telephone inquiries may be made by calling:

(214) 423-0090

CONTENTS

? Font + Underline   Cntrl - F8
Subscript, Superscript   under 1. Size

Suppress! This page etc.

WORDPERFECT 5.1 UPDATE

1

INTRODUCTION

Welcome to WordPerfect!

WordPerfect 5.0/5.1 is a word processing program which is used with an IBM-compatible computer. The computer functions as a body and WordPerfect like a brain enabling the user to perform key word processing operations.

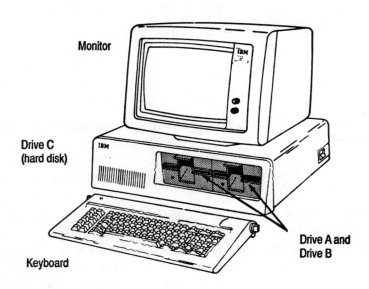

The computer screen is called a *monitor*. It is basically like a television screen. Most monitors are monochrome, meaning one color (usually amber, gray, or green) on a black or dark gray background. Some monitors are color and allow the user to choose colors by preference.

Below the monitor is the *computer* where the *disk drives* are located.

Disks

Disks look like this:

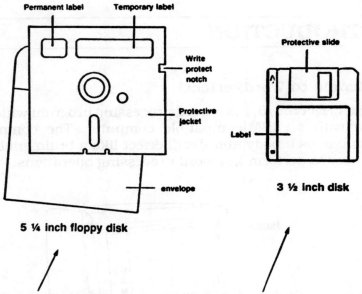

Permanent label   Temporary label

Write protect notch

Protective jacket

envelope

5 ¼ inch floppy disk

Protective slide

Label

3 ½ inch disk

Load vertical line of film forward, labeled side up.

Load metal rectangle forward, labeled side up.

There are several types of IBM-compatible personal computers:

- **Hard Drive** In this instance, the software (or the "program") is already loaded on the computer which houses an internal location for saved work called C: drive. In addition, there is a visible disk drive on the front of the computer where work disks may be inserted (called A: drive).

- **Dual Floppy** With a dual floppy computer, the software must be loaded by disk from the A: and B: drives *after* first loading the DOS disk on the system from drive A:.

In front of the computer is the *keyboard*. Basic typewriter keys remain the same, except that to the left or above the letter keys are the WordPerfect *function keys* with a surrounding *template* of commands and submenus. To the right of the letter keys are the *scrolling arrow keys* which are used to move around a typed document.

2

START-UP/HELP FEATURE

In order to load WordPerfect and begin using its word processing features, it is first necessary to turn on the computer and "boot" the system. ("Boot" is a computer term for loading the operating system.) There will be a butterfly switch either on the right side, back, or front of the computer, and likewise on the monitor.

Loading WordPerfect on a Dual Floppy Computer

Insert the DOS disk into the A: drive and flip the switches on.

After DOS loads, you will be prompted with:

ENTER NEW DATE:
Example: (02-14-91)

Type in the current date and press **Return** (or **Enter**). You will then be prompted with:

ENTER NEW TIME:

You may skip this prompt by pressing **Return**.

Remove the DOS disk after the following appears:

A>

Insert the WordPerfect Program Disk No. 1 in drive A and No. 2 in drive B. Close the latches. At the A> prompt, type **wp** and press **Return**. The WordPerfect trademark will then flash across the screen. After the program has loaded, a virtually blank screen will appear. At this time, remove WordPerfect Program Disk No. 1 and replace it with a work disk and close the latch. Leave WordPerfect Program Disk No. 2 in drive B at all times.

NOTE

If using new, previously unused work disks, it will be necessary to format them. Please refer to the addendum for formatting procedures.

Loading WordPerfect on a Hard Drive

If WordPerfect has been installed on the hard disk, it may be accessed in a number of ways. Once switched on, your computer may be programmed to immediately load WordPerfect. In this instance, it will blink and flash numerous messages across the screen before it displays the starting screen.

If your computer does not load WordPerfect immediately upon startup, it may show the following prompt:

C:\>

In this instance, WordPerfect may be loaded from a batch file (a file that contains a list of operations the computer performs) on the hard disk. The batch file name must be typed at the DOS prompt. Some common names for batch files are: WORD, DATA, WP50, or WP.

If you do not know which word to type, experiment by typing one of the names and pressing **Return** at the C:\> prompt.

A third possible method for loading WordPerfect is selecting the menu choice from a programmed menu screen, which gives numerous choices laid out by letters for the different software programs available on that given computer. In this case, you would simply select the letter for the WordPerfect program and press **Return**.

After WordPerfect has loaded and the WordPerfect trademark screen has flashed over the screen, the WordPerfect starting screen appears. It is a blank screen with the *cursor* at the top left corner and the *status line* in the bottom right corner.

The menu tA program to come on.

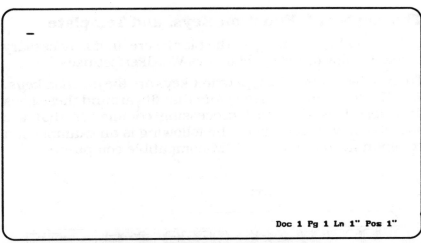

Doc 1 Pg 1 Ln 1" Pos 1"

WordPerfect starting screen with cursor and status line.

The status line describes the cursor position and document status. To the left of the status line is where the function key submenu prompts will appear. Please note that you are in Document 1, on Page 1, and on Line 1. WordPerfect has default margins set at one inch on all sides. Line 1" means that the default top and bottom margins are set to begin printing one inch from the top of the page and to stop one inch from the bottom. Pos 1" means that the margins are set at 1" on each side of the page.

The Keyboard, Function Keys, and Template

Before you begin typing on the blank screen, it is necessary to learn a few of the special keys WordPerfect uses.

To the left or above the typewriter keys are the *function keys*. WordPerfect supplies a *template* that fits around these keys and describes the word processing commands that are associated with each key. The following is an example of a common keyboard on an IBM-compatible computer:

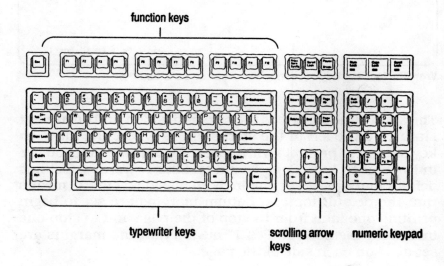

function keys

typewriter keys   scrolling arrow keys   numeric keypad

In addition to the function keys, WordPerfect uses several special keys to access commands. They are *Ctrl*, *Shift*, and *Alt*. These keys are pressed simultaneously with a function key.

The function key template is color coded to indicate function key, Ctrl function key, Shift function key and Alt function key sequences.

Press the function key or key combination to access the WordPerfect command.

	Red	Green	Blue	Black
	Ctrl-function	Shift-function	Alt-function	Function key
F1	Shell	SETUP	Thesaurus	Cancel
F2	Spell	LEFT SEARCH	Replace	Search Right
F3	Screen	SWITCH	Reveal Codes	Help
F4	Move	L/R INDENT	Block	Right Indent
F5	Text In/Out	DATE/OUTLINE	Mark Text	List Files
F6	Tab Align	CENTER	Flush Right	Bold
F7	Footnote	PRINT	Math/Columns	Exit
F8	Font	FORMAT	Style	Underline
F9	Merge/Sort	MERGE CODES	Graphics	Merge R
F10	Macro Define	RETRIEVE	Macro	Save

[Handwritten annotations: "F8 Font" circled; "END FIELD" next to F9 Merge R; below table: "F11 REVEAL ~ Alt F3   F12 BLOCK (~ Alt F4)"]

To the right of the typewriter keyboard are the *scrolling arrow keys*. They may be located on the 10-key pad, or on some keyboards, they may be located in an area between the typewriter keys and the 10-key pad. You will see little arrows on the keys. These keys allow you to scroll around the typed text on screen. If you were to press **Return** (or **Enter**) to move down a page of text (like on a standard typewriter) extra lines and open spaces would be created. The scrolling arrow keys must be used instead.

Above the 10-key pad is a *Num Lock* key. When that key is pressed and the light is on, the 10-key pad can only be used to type numbers. *Num Lock* is one of the keyboard keys known as a "toggle" key because it is used in an on/off fashion. Press it once, you'll turn it on. Press it again, and you'll turn it back off. If the *Num Lock* is on, you will notice that in your status line on the bottom of the screen, "Pos" will be flashing on and off. When you press *Num Lock* to take it off, "Pos" will no longer be flashing.

TURN THE NUM LOCK KEY OFF.

Looking over the keyboard, you will also see several other toggle keys (keys which are used in an on/off fashion) that are also displayed in the status line.

Caps Lock allows you to type all in caps, with the added bonus of typing numbers and punctuation without having to release the shift (caps) lock key.

Ins located on the zero key in the 10-key pad allows you to toggle between insert or "typeover." It is best to leave this key off and use the arrow keys, Backspace and Delete to edit existing text.

NOTE

Backspace erases to the left of the cursor. *Delete* erases where the cursor presently is and to the right.

For example, type:

Your Name

then press the **Left Arrow** four times. Now type:

WordPerfect holds text to the right.

As you can see, the last four letters of your name move to the right of the phrase as you are typing. By leaving the Ins on, you will establish more consistent work habits and speed in editing.

Backspace and *Delete* are the keys used to erase text.

Press **Backspace** several times until the phrase "Word-Perfect holds text to the right" is deleted.

Now, press **Delete** four times. You will see that you have deleted the last four letters of your name. Now re-type those four letters of your name.

Help Function Key Support Feature

WordPerfect offers a support feature which provides descriptive definitions for each template function. This feature is called *Help* and is located on F3 of the function key pad.

As a new user, you can easily access Help from any working position, in or out of a document. If you need help understanding functions on the template, the Help feature is a quick and concise reference tool.

EXERCISE: Accessing the Help Feature Menu

Press **F3** (Help). WordPerfect now displays the following screen:

```
  Help                                          WP 5.0    05/05/88


        Press any letter to get an alphabetical list of features.

           The list will include the features that start with that letter,
           along with the name of the key where the feature is found.   You
           can then press that key to get a description of how the feature
           works.

        Press any function key to get information about the use of the key.

           Some keys may let you choose from a menu to get more information
           about various options.   Press HELP again to display the template.

        Press Enter or Space bar to exit Help.



```

Help starting screen

WordPerfect Help also offers an alphabetical list of features when you type the first letter of a word. This feature is helpful when you know what function you would like to perform but cannot remember how to access it on the template.

While still in the Help menu type **S**. The following screen listing will appear:

```
Key           Feature                              Key Name

F10           Save Text                            Save
Ctrl-F3       Screen                               Screen
+(Num Pad)    Screen Down                          Screen Down
-(Num Pad)    Screen Up                            Screen Up
Shft-F1       Screen Setup                         Setup,3
Alt-F2        Search and Replace                   Replace
F5            Search for Text in File(s)           List Files,9
Ctrl-F9       Secondary File, Merge                Merge/Sort
Alt-F3        See Codes                            Reveal Codes
Shft-F7       Select Printer(s)                    Print
Shft-F8       Set Pitch (Letter/Word Spacing)      Format,4,6,3
Ctrl-F8       Shadow Print                         Font,2
Shft-F7       Send Printer a "GO"                  Print,4
Shft-F7       Sheet Feeder                         Print,S,3
Alt-F5        Short Form, Table of Auth.           Mark Text,4
Shft-F1       Side-by-side Columns Display         Setup,3
Ctrl-F8       Size of Print                        Font
Ctrl-F8       Small Capitalized Print              Font,2
Ctrl-F8       Small Print                          Font,1
Ctrl "-"      Soft Hyphen                          Soft Hyphen

              Type 1 for more help: 0
```

Help features beginning with the letter "s."

As you can see by the extensive selections which are available, **F3** (Help) is an excellent reference tool for the beginning user.

Press **Enter** or the **Spacebar** to exit the Help feature.

If you would like an extended definition of a template function, WordPerfect Help offers easily accessed reference.

EXERCISE: Accessing the Help Feature Function Key Definitions

Press **F3** (Help). Then press **Shift F6** (Center). The Word-Perfect *Help* feature now displays the following screen:

```
Center

     Centers one or several lines between margins or over columns.

Between margins
     a.  To center a line, place the cursor at the left margin and press
         Center.  Any text typed will automatically be centered until Tab or
         Enter is pressed.
     b.  With an existing line of text, press Center at the beginning of the
         line.  The line will be centered after down arrow is pressed.

Over columns
     a.  Over a text column, press Center at the column's left margin and
         type the text.
     a.  Over a column created with tabs or indents, tab to where you want
         the text centered, press Center and type the text.

Several lines can be centered by blocking the text then pressing Center.
```

Help feature's Shift F6 (Center) definitions.

Please notice that the WordPerfect Help screen now shows information which explains the Center function.

Press **Enter** or the **Spacebar** to exit the Help feature.

3

EXERCISE AND BEGINNING APPLICATION

To help you become accustomed to the WordPerfect keyboard, please type the following document entitled *The Secret of Success*. You will be given various template/ function key instructions as you go along. You will notice that throughout the document there are spelling errors. LEAVE ALL ERRORS. They are needed for the editing exercises in following sections.

NOTE

Do not press Return or Enter at the end of each line in a paragraph as you would on a standard typewriter. WordPerfect "wraps" the text to the next line for you so that you can type without having to stop and make line-end decisions!

EXERCISE: Center, Underline, Bold, Caps Lock, Tabs, Left-Right Indent, Left Indent

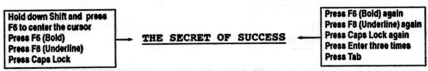

Hold down Shift and press F6 to center the cursor
Press F6 (Bold)
Press F8 (Underline)
Press Caps Lock

→ THE SECRET OF SUCCESS ←

Press F6 (Bold) again
Press F8 (Underline) again
Press Caps Lock again
Press Enter three times
Press Tab

Succeed means "to have something turn out well," or "to attain a desired object or end." Some people desire to succeed yet also fear success at the same time. This state is termed as "ambivalence," which is defined in Webster's as "simultaneous attraction toward and repulsion from an object, person or

action." Another definition for ambivalence is
"uncertainty as to which approach to follow."

Press Tab

Press Return twice

Press F6

Press F8

Upon seeing another person who is successful,
many will call it "luck." Luck has less to do with
success than effort. Success is the fruit of thought,
purpose and action. One must obtain an objective,

Press F6

mentaally draw up plans, and work every day towards
that goal. At the same time, it is important to
constantly visualize having achieved the goal.
Positive visualization stamps FAITH on the
subconscious. Perseverence assures the end result:
SUCCESS.

Press Return twice

Press Tab

Remember the three basic principles to be applied
to any goal, whether it be to complete a list of
household chores, find a better paying job, learn a
new skill, or better your lifestyle: Thought, Purpose
and Action.

Press Return twice

**Press Shift-F4
(Left-Right Indent)
three times**

"When you have eliminated the
impossible, whatever remains,
however improbable, ...must be
the truth." **Press Return**
Sherlocck Hollmes

Press Return twice

Press F6

Press Tab

Success is the result of COMPLETION, so DON'T
STOP. Keep practicing and find accomplisshment in

Press F6

each day, for the true secret of success is that it
already belongs to you. No one wakes up one day and
says, "Ah, at last I have success — it is written
right here on my forehead — Hurray!"

Press Return twice

**Press
F4 (Left
Indent)**

Success is the constsant of every positive thing
you think, say and do. Even failure is a form of
success, for the positive lessons learned correct
the effort, and ultimately brings one to the
attainment of dreams.

Press Return twice

Good luck!

Press Return

NOTE

Proceed to the next section for beginner's
editing.

The completed text looks like this when printed:

THE SECRET OF SUCCESS

Succeed means "to have something turn out well," or "to attain a desired object or end." Some people desire to succeed, yet also fear success at the same time. This state is termed as "ambivalence," which is defined in Webster's as "simultaneous attraction toward and repulsion from an object, person or action." Another definition for ambivalence is "uncertainty as to which approach to follow."

Upon seeing another person who is successful, many will call it "luck." Luck has less to do with success than <u>effort</u>. Success is the fruit of **thought, purpose and action**. One must obtain an objective, mentally draw up plans, and work every day towards that goal. At the same time, it is important to constantly visualize having achieved the goal. Positive visualization stamps FAITH on the subconscious. Perseverance assures the end result: SUCCESS.

Remember the three basic principles to be applied to any goal, whether it be to complete a list of household chores, find a better paying job, learn a new skill, or better your lifestyle: Thought, Purpose and Action.

"When you have eliminated the impossible, whatever remains, however improbable, ... must be the truth."
Sherlock Holmes

Success is the result of COMPLETION, so DON'T STOP. Keep practicing and find accomplishment in each day, for the true secret of success is that it already belongs to you. No one wakes up one day and says, "Ah, at last I have success -- it is written right here on my forehead -- Hurray!"

Success is the constant of every positive thing you think, say and do. Even <u>failure</u> is a form of success, for the positive lessons learned correct the effort, and ultimately brings one to the attainment of dreams.

Good luck!

? FONTS

4

BEGINNER'S EDITING

Utilizing WordPerfect's editing features can cut revision time in half, making the tedious job of editing easier, faster, and more productive.

One of the most crucial aspects of editing is the speed at which the user can move the cursor to a desired word or phrase. Next in importance is the speed by which WordPerfect erasure (deletion) and replacement of correct text can be applied.

As you proceed through the following WordPerfect editing exercise, please pay special attention to the cursor movement methods.

EXERCISE: Up/Down/Right/Left, Word-by-Word Cursor Movement, and Speed Tips

Using the **Up Arrow** (8 on the keypad), move the cursor to the beginning of the first paragraph. Hold down the **Ctrl** key and press the **Right Arrow** (6 on the keypad) several times. You will notice that on the screen, the cursor is moving word-by-word now, instead of letter-by-letter. Hold down the **Ctrl** key and press **Left Arrow** (4 on the keypad) to move the cursor to the left, word-by-word.

NOTE

You may also hold down the scrolling arrow key to accelerate the cursor.

Continue moving around the screen to the bottom of the file. Press **Up Arrow** to place the cursor under the "s" in "conststant." Press **Del** (bottom of 10-key pad) to delete the letter.

NOTE

Remember that Backspace erases to the left of the cursor; Delete erases where the cursor presently is and to the right. As you scroll the page by pressing Down Arrow, WordPerfect automatically reformats the paragraphs for you so that there are no large gaps in the text.

5

SPELL CHECK

WordPerfect has an exceptional spell check program which scans the document, highlighting a misspelling and offering a choice of the correct spelling in its place.

Gone are the days of "typos" in a spell-checked document. As advanced as the spell check is, it is nonetheless necessary to read over a document for accuracy. The spell check does not recognize word usage errors such as "on" instead of "in."

The following exercise will familiarize you with the performance features of the spell check. Take time to examine each step and to experiment with further selections in the spelling menu.

EXERCISE: Beginning the Spell Check

Press **Pg Up** (9 on the keypad). Hold down **Ctrl** and press **F2** once to access the spell check.

The following screen appears with the spell check menu at the bottom of the screen:

```
                    THE SECRET OF SUCCESS

         Succeed means "to have something turn out well." or "to
attain a desired object or end." Some people desire to succeed, yet
also fear success at the same time. This state is termed as
"ambivalence," which is defined in Webster's as "simultaneous
attraction toward and repulssion from an object, person or action."
Another definition for ambivalence is "uncertainty as to which
approach to follow."

         Upon seeing another person who is successful, many will
call it "luck." Luck has less to do with success than effort.
Success is the fruit of thought, purpose and action. One must
obtain an objective, mentaally draw up plans, and work every day
towards that goal. At the same time, it is important to constantly
visualize having achieved the goal. Positive visualization stamps
FAITH on the subconscious. Perseverence assures the end result:
SUCCESS.

         Remember the three basic principles to be apploied to any
goal, whether it be to complete a list of household chores, find
a better paying job, learn a new skill, or better your lifestyle:
Thought, Purpose and Action.
Check: 1 Word; 2 Page; 3 Document; 4 New Sup. Dictionary; 5 Look Up; 6 Count: 0
```

Ctrl F2 - Spell Check Menu

The most commonly used choices are: "2 Page" or "3 Document." Most often, a spelling check is conducted *after completing a letter, document, or paper.* Therefore, "3 Document" is the logical, general choice. You need not be concerned with the other selections for your basic training. In time, if you would like to utilize more of WordPerfect, the other options may be explored.

NOTE

Before continuing with the spell check, please read the following spell check information.

When WordPerfect locates a misspelled (or seemingly misspelled) word, you will be prompted with the following type of screen:

```
          Succeed means "to have something turn out well," or "to
     attain a desired object or end." Some people desire to succeed, yet
     also fear success at the same time. This state is termed as
     "ambivalence," which is defined in Webster's as "simultaneous
     attraction toward and repulssion from an object, person or action."
     Another definition for ambivalence is "uncertainty as to which
     approach to follow."

          Upon seeing another person who is successful, many will
     call it "luck." Luck has less to do with success than effort.

     ====================================================================

     A. repulsion




     Not Found: 1 Skip Once; 2 Skip; 3 Add Word; 4 Edit; 5 Look Up:  0
```

Ctrl F2 - Spell check in operation

Choosing the Correct Spelling by Letter

If the highlighted misspelling is a common word in the dictionary, WordPerfect will provide a list of possible correct spellings set off by letters of the alphabet. Choose the letter corresponding with the correct word. WordPerfect will then replace the misspelling with the correct word and continue to search for other misspelled words.

Adding Commonly Used Words to the Dictionary

If a city, name, or word is not listed in the dictionary and is highlighted as a misspelling, even though it is not misspelled, you may choose to add it to the dictionary by typing 3 (Add Word).

Skipping Over Correct Words the Dictionary Doesn't Recognize

If the word or name highlighted is not actually a misspelling, (the basic dictionary doesn't recognize names and abbreviations) type 2 (Skip) to skip over it.

Editing a Misspelling Yourself

If WordPerfect highlights a misspelled word but cannot locate the proper spelling in its dictionary, it will be necessary to type the correct spelling yourself by typing 4 (Edit). The cursor will then be positioned at the misspelling. Remember to look over the entire screen for WordPerfect's prompts to guide you to starting positions. You will need to press F7 (Exit) when finished editing the word.

End of Spell Check

Once WordPerfect is finished with the spell check, you will be prompted with the following:

Word Count: Press any key to continue

At this point, you would press Return and the spell check procedure would be complete.

EXERCISE: Spell Check (continued)

Proceed with the spell check by typing **3** (Document).

WordPerfect will now begin searching for misspelled words in your document. Refer to the previous paragraphs if necessary to complete the spell check.

When the spell check is completed, WordPerfect counts all words in the document. Press any key (**Return** or **Enter**) to end the spell check and continue working on the document.

6

SAVING WORK

The single most important aspect of word processing is the capability of the user to save work on disk. Saving the work ensures that it can be easily recalled and revised, thus eliminating the need to retype the document.

In the following exercise, you will learn that there are two ways to save a document. One way is to save the document on the screen through **F10** (Save). The document would then remain on screen after being saved, and the name of the saved document would appear at the bottom left of the screen. The second way to save is by exiting the document. Both methods are commonly used and require that several prompts be followed. For this reason, losing a document is quite unlikely.

You will want to SAVE this exercise on your work disk or on the hard disk so that it can be accessed in the future for any necessary changes or reprints.

Since Save is listed in black on the bottom of the F10 function key template, there will be no need to press a control key. You would first be prompted with:

Document to be saved: a:

a:, b:, or c: indicates the location where your work will be saved. The letter is followed by a colon (:) so the computer is able to translate that you are referring to a location. On a hard disk, the internal drive is "c," and if work is stored on "c," a work disk won't be needed. However, if you do choose to save the document on a work disk, insert a work disk into the disk drive. This drive will be referred to as drive A.

Up to eight letters can be used for the document name.

NOTE

Longer names can be used if working with WordPerfect 5.1. Please refer to the 5.1 Update section for further reference.

A short three-letter description may also be inserted after the name by using a period in the title. Example:

Document to be saved: c:\thompson.ltr

in full   c:\WP51\Doc\thompson.ltr

NOTE

Do not insert a backslash (\). The computer does this for you.

Notice that the title is typed in lowercase letters. Make a habit of not capitalizing at prompts. The computer will do this for you.

EXERCISE: F10 (Save)

Press **F10** (Save).

Depending upon where you want to save your work, type either a:, b:, or c: (followed by a colon as indicated) and type the following name for your work:

your-doc.ltr

NOTE

Do not press the Spacebar while typing the title of your work. If a template command is given by accident or problems occur and there is a need to cancel, press F1 (Cancel) and start over with the function key command.

Now, press **Return** (or **Enter**). The following prompt appears in the bottom left of your screen:

Saving c:\your-doc.ltr

Your document is now saved on the disk.

Introduction to Subsidiary Directories

When using a hard drive it is sometimes necessary to save, retrieve, or create a subdirectory (branch) of the default directory (the place on the hard drive generally referred to as c: or WP50). Please refer to Section 11, List Files, 7 Other Directory for further information about saving and retrieving documents in subsidiary directories.

7

PRINTERS

WordPerfect drives a variety of printers used at home or in the office:

Laser: This printer is like a copier in that it accepts the image and copies it on paper with heat and toner.

Dot Matrix: On a dot matrix printer, the letters are printed on the paper with a series of pins striking the ink ribbon.

Daisy Wheel: On a daisy wheel printer, the letters are printed like on a typewriter, by a daisy wheel letter striking the ink ribbon.

When WordPerfect is installed, the printer selection is made for your computer.

Usually there is a butterfly switch on the side or back of the printer. **Flip the switch on**. Notice that on all printers, there is an "on line" light. If that light is off, the printer will not print. Make sure this light is on. If there is continuous-feed paper already loaded, then you don't need to concern yourself with loading the paper. If you are loading individual sheets, line the paper into the printer and feed it in at this time.

8

PRINTING A DOCUMENT ON THE SCREEN

Though there are several ways to print a document, the following exercise will familiarize you with printing the document *presently on your screen* and with the selections available in the Print Format menu.

EXERCISE: Shift F7 (Print)

Hold down **Shift** and press **F7**. You will see the following:

```
Print

        1 - Full Document
        2 - Page
        3 - Document on Disk
        4 - Control Printer
        5 - Type Through
        6 - View Document
        7 - Initialize Printer

Options

        S - Select Printer          Star NX-1000
        B - Binding                 0"
        N - Number of Copies        1
        G - Graphics Quality        Medium
        T - Text Quality            High




    Selection: 0
```

Shift F7 - Print Format Menu

Type **2** for Page.

At this time, the page should print.

Let's pretend that, for some reason, the page is not printing. Press **Shift F7** (Print). Type **4** (Control Printer). WordPerfect displays a screen similar to the following:

```
Print: Control Printer

Current Job

Job Number: None                              Page Number:  None
Status:     No print jobs                     Current Copy: None
Message:    None
Paper:      None
Location:   None
Action:     None


Job List

Job  Document              Destination        Print Options




Additional Jobs Not Shown: 0


1 Cancel Job(s); 2 Rush Job; 3 Display Jobs; 4 Go (start printer); 5 Stop: 0
```

Shift F7 - Control Printer Menu

Here you can see if the computer accepted your print command. If no job is listed, then press **F1** to cancel the command and return to the document on screen. Repeat the **Shift F7** command. If a job is listed, then see if there are any messages indicating why your document might not be printing. If all seems to be right, then double-check to see if the printer **on-line** light is on. If it is, sometimes giving the computer a boost is all that is necessary. You can achieve this by choosing **4** in the Control Printer menu to tell the printer "GO!"

9

EXITING FROM THE SCREEN AND RESAVING

As stated earlier, there are two ways to save a document. We used *Save* (F10). Now that you have successfully saved and printed the document, you will want to clear your screen and proceed to a new project. WordPerfect offers the opportunity for saving (or re-saving) as you *Exit* the document on the screen. This is a protective measure to remind you if you haven't already saved your document, to do so at this time.

EXERCISE: Screen Exit and Prompts

Press **F7** (Exit). WordPerfect displays the following prompt:

Save Document? (Y/N) Yes

In this situation, you know that you have already saved the document. However, perhaps you might like to save it again, just to be sure. Since the computer is already prompting with a "yes" as the default, just press **Return**. The screen now displays:

Document to be saved: c:\your-doc.ltr

Press **Return**.

WordPerfect now prompts with:

Replace c:\your-doc.ltr? (Y/N) No

Type **Y** for yes. Stop a moment and consider why. Your work disk is similar to a cassette tape. You must record *over* the other material. In order to re-save your document, you must replace the "old" text with the "new." The computer will re-save over the previous spot on the disk because it is being saved again under the same name.

Please note that the computer now prompts with:

Exit WP? (Y/N) No   **(Cancel to return to Document)**

The computer now asks if you desire to exit WordPerfect (for the day). Type **N** (No) since you want to proceed with new work. After these steps, the WordPerfect starting screen is displayed.

NOTE

At the end of the day you press **F7** (Exit) and type **Y** (Yes) so that the system can shut down.

10

DATE CODE/FORMAT

WordPerfect's *Date/Outline* option offers automatic date insertion. This feature is a big timesaver, as well as an error-saving device in the daily generation of voluminous office correspondence.

EXERCISE: Letter Including Ctrl F5 (Date) Insertion

Type the letter exercise below:

Press **Shift F6** (Center).

Press **Shift F5** (Date/Outline)

Type **1** (Date Text).

Press **Return** four times.

Type the following letter.

Ms. Darlene Worthe
Office Manager
Smith & Williams
34 Honor Circle
Suite 1480
Dallas, Texas

Dear Ms. Worthe:

    Enclosed, please find the outline requested by Mr. Dietrich in your Dallas office.

If you have any questions, please do not hesitate to contact me.

Sincerely,

Julie Price
Systems Coordinator

As you can see, WordPerfect inserted the date, alleviating tedious, repetitive date-typing throughout the day.

WordPerfect took the *Date* feature one step further by introducing *Date Code*. *Date Code* prevents one of the most frequent daily errors in an office: forgetting to change the date of a draft document to the present day's date.

EXERCISE: Date Code

Move the cursor back to the left margin on the date line in the letter above.

Press **Ctrl End** to delete the entire line.

Press **Shift F5** (Date/Outline).

Type **2** (Date Code).

Press **Down Arrow** to adjust format.

Today's date is still inserted like before, but if the letter were to be revised over the next few days, the next time the letter was retrieved for revisions, the date would automatically adjust to the present day's date, rather than the original date of draft.

Press **F7** (Exit), type **N** (do not save) and **N** (do not exit WP) to clear the screen.

11

LIST FILES

List Files lists in alphabetical order all saved documents on a hard drive or work disk. List Files acts basically as a table of contents or "directory" of the documents as well as providing a menu for retrieving, deleting, renaming, printing, and copying.

EXERCISE: Accessing List Files

Press **F5** (List Files). You will be prompted with:

Dir A:*.*

Dir B:*.*

or

Dir C:*.*

With a blinking cursor under the letter.

If the desired location letter is already displayed, press **Return** or **Enter**. If the location letter displayed is incorrect, type the letter corresponding to the location where your work is stored, and press **Return** or **Enter**. WordPerfect displays a screen similar to the following:

```
08/19/90  07:27          Directory C:\WP50\CO  ESI\*.*
Document size:        0  Free:   3151872  Used:    13552        Files:  10

  . <CURRENT>    <DIR>                      .. <PARENT>   <DIR>
JDT      .      <DIR>    08/19/90 07:27    RVW      .     <DIR>    08/19/90 07:27
BI-YEARL.RPT     1694    08/19/90 07:28    JONES    .LTR   1694    08/19/90 07:28
MYERS   .LTR     1694    08/19/90 07:29    QUARTLY  .RPT   1694    08/19/90 07:30
RENAULDO.LTR     1694    08/19/90 07:31    SUMMER   .BBQ   1694    08/19/90 07:32
TRANSCON.PRO     1694    08/19/90 07:33    XMASLIST.INV   1694    08/19/90 07:34




    1 Retrieve; 2 Delete; 3 Move/Rename; 4 Print; 5 Text In;
    6 Look; 7 Other Directory; 8 Copy; 9 Word Search; N Name Search: 6
```

F5 - List Files Menu

The List Files menu displays the following options at the bottom of the screen:

1 Retrieve Brings a copy of the document of choice back to the screen for revisions. Retrieve can also be used to insert a copy of one file into another file at the current cursor location.

2 Delete Allows you to delete or erase a particular document. To delete a document type **2** and WordPerfect prompts with:

Delete B:\doc-name? (Y/N) No

This confirming question reminds you that you are permanently deleting the file and lets you change your mind by typing any key other than Y to perform the deletion. This option should only be used when you are *absolutely certain* that the document won't be needed again.

3 Move/Rename Allows a document to be renamed. If you wanted to give a new title to an existing document, you would type **3** (Move/Rename) and would be prompted with:

New name: B:\doc-name

At this time, you would simply type a new name for the document and the new name would replace the previous name in the List Files directory.

4 Print Allows you to print one or more files directly from the List Files directory. This is a timesaver, especially if a document is lengthy. When printing a document from List Files, you could press **F1** (Cancel) to clear the List Files menu from the screen and begin typing a new document.

5 Text In Retrieves ASCII files.

6 Look Allows you to "peek" at a document to make sure it is definitely the one you need without having to take the extra time to retrieve, exit, and list files to retrieve again. Look can also be used to display the files in a directory.

NOTE
You cannot work on the document while in the "6" Look mode.

7 Other Directory Is used for creating subdirectories or changing the default directory.

When using a hard drive it will sometimes be necessary to save, retrieve, or create a subdirectory (branch) of the default directory (the place on the hard disk generally referred to as C: or WP50).

When a listed file in the List Files table of contents is followed by <DIR>, this means the file is a subdirectory.

The following is a tree illustrating the basic theorem of subsidiary directories:

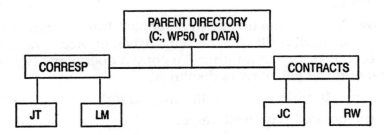

Example of Individualized Branches of Parent Directory

EXERCISE: Creating a Subdirectory

If you would like to create a subdirectory which will be used solely for correspondence, press **F5** (List Files) and type **7**. You will be prompted with:

New directory: = c:

(and the parent directory, i.e., WP50 or DATA)

Type **c:\\(your parent directory)\\corresp** and press **Return**.

NOTE

Be sure to type a backslash (\\), not a forward slash (/).

You will then be prompted with:

Create c:\\wp50\\corresp? (Y/N) No

Type **Y** and press **Return**.

Now you will note that there is a new directory listed in List Files which is a subsidiary of the parent default directory. From this point on, save all correspondence under that directory.

When listing files for a subdirectory, move the highlight bar to the desired directory and press **Return** twice. That will take you into the subsidiary table of contents of text work or revisions.

8 Copy Allows a document to be copied from one disk to another, or from a disk to the hard drive, or vice-versa, or from one directory to another. To copy a document type **8** (Copy) and the following is displayed:

Copy this file to:_ {blinking cursor}

Type the desired path and name.

9 Word Search Marks files in the List Files directory. This option decreases searching time by defining certain conditions for marking files. Files can be marked with an asterisk for mass usage. For example, if you were going to delete five or ten documents, you could move the highlight bar to the desired files, type an asterisk beside each one, and then type **2** (Delete). WordPerfect then prompts you with the following backup question:

Delete marked files? Y/N

Upon typing **Y**, all of the marked files are erased.

NOTE

It is, however, advisable that you do not attempt to utilize this feature until you are very comfortable with WordPerfect and can be absolutely sure that the files you have marked should be deleted.

N Name Search Is a timesaver. Rather than scroll through List Files line-by-line (which can become quite tedious) WordPerfect offers a name searching option that enables you to deliver the cursor in the vicinity (or directly on) a desired file. You type **N**, then begin typing the name of the desired document. Once the highlight bar is delivered to any files bearing that or a similar name, you press **Enter** and make the file/menu selection.

The Up, Down, Right and Left Arrow keys move the highlight bar over the document titles in the List Files directory. You use this highlight bar to indicate which document(s) you want to access for performing List Files menu functions.

EXERCISE: Retrieving Your Document

Since you are presently in List Files, move the highlight bar with the arrow keys until "your-doc" is highlighted.

Type **1** (Retrieve) **"your-doc."**

WordPerfect displays the document.

12

REVEAL CODES

Reveal Codes is actually like an "x-ray" of the document showing each and every keystroke and command. It can be utilized for checking formatting codes and deleting unwanted commands from the document, such as UND, BOLD, or INDENT.

EXERCISE: Accessing Reveal Codes

At the very top of "your-doc," press **Alt F3** (Reveal Codes). As you can see below, the screen is divided horizontally with a line showing the margins and tabs. WordPerfect separates the actual document at the top of the page from the "x-ray" of the document beneath it.

```
                        THE SECRET OF SUCCESS


             Succeed means "to have something turn out well," or "to
        attain a desired object or end." Some people desire to succeed,
        yet also fear success at the same time. This state is termed as
        "ambivalence," which is defined in Webster's as "simultaneous
        attraction toward and repulsion from an object, person or
        action." Another definition for ambivalence is "uncertainty as to
        which approach to follow."

        C:\WP50\CORRESP\YOUR-DOC.LTR                    Doc 1 Pg 1 Ln 1" Pos 1"
        [                                               ]
        [Cntr][BOLD][UND]THE SECRET OF SUCCESS[bold][und][C/A/Flrt][HRt]
        [HRt]
        [HRt]
        [Tab][Tab]Succeed means "to have something turn out well," or "to[SRt]
        attain a desired object or end." Some people desire to succeed,[SRt]
        yet also fear success at the same time. This state is termed as[SRt]
        "ambivalence," which is defined in Webster's as "simultaneous[SRt]
        attraction toward and repulsion from an object, person or[SRt]
        action." Another definition for ambivalence is "uncertainty as to[SRt]
        which approach to follow."[HRt]

        Press Reveal Codes to restore screen
```

Alt F3 - Reveal Codes

Either look at the actual document above the dividing bar, or look below the dividing bar. **Do not attempt to look at the full screen.** Below the bar you will see numerous abbreviations. In Reveal Codes, your cursor is actually a highlight on one of the commands.

Reveal Codes Language

Now, walk through each of the following paragraphs to examine and translate Reveal Codes language.

Directly below the Reveal Codes dividing line, you should see:

[Font: Courier 10 pitch] indicates an optional type/font style setting that may or may not be on your *Reveal Codes* screen.

[Cntr] signaling that you have told the computer to center the text. The **[C/A/Flrt]** shows the centering ended by pressing **Return** [HRt].

Continuing, please note that the beginning of underlining is indicated with **[UND]** (begin underline) and **[und]** (end underline).

The **Bold** command is indicated with **[BOLD]** (begin bold) and **[bold]** (end bold).

[C/A/Flrt] shows the end of centering before a carriage return.

[HRt] stands for hard return meaning that you, the user, pressed **Return** rather than letting the computer make line-end decisions and "wrap the text around" to the next line for you. When the computer makes line-end decisions, it inserts a soft return which is indicated by **[SRt]**.

[Tab] indicates a tab of 5 spaces was inserted.

[→Indent←] shows that the text will be indented in increments of five spaces from *both the right and left* margins. You indicate how many five-space indents should occur by consecutively pressing **Shift F4** (→Indent←) as many times as necessary.

[→**Indent**] shows that the text will be held to the indented left margin in increments of five spaces, achieved by consecutively pressing the **F4** (→Indent) key as many times (in increments of five spaces) as necessary.

Press **Alt F3** (Reveal Codes) to remove reveal codes from the screen (as it acts as a toggle (on/off) key).

13

BLOCKING (HIGHLIGHTING) TEXT MOVING/COPYING/DELETING/ UNDELETING BLOCKED TEXT

There will be times when you need to manipulate entire lines, paragraphs, and pages. In order for WordPerfect to interpret what text needs special attention, you must first *Block* (highlight) the text you would like to do something with.

EXERCISE: Block Underlining, Block Bolding, Block Moving, Block Deleting, Block Undeleting

Using the arrow keys, move the cursor to the first letter of the beginning word in the first paragraph.

Press **Alt F4** (Block). Please notice that in the bottom left-hand corner of your screen, *Block On* is flashing. Now, press **Ctrl Right Arrow** to move the cursor to the right a few words. Now press **Down Arrow** and move the block (highlight) down to the last line of the paragraph. (This can also be achieved by pressing **Return** or **Enter**. After reaching the last line, press **End** (on the 10-keypad) and the cursor will then move to the *end of that line* in the paragraph.

Now that you have blocked (highlighted) the text, it is now time to instruct WordPerfect to do something with it.

With **Block On** still blinking, press **F8** (Underline). You will note that the paragraph which you blocked is now underlined.

Move the cursor back up to the first letter of the beginning word in the first paragraph. Press **Alt F4** (Block) and move the cursor with the arrow keys until you have again highlighted a sentence or paragraph.

Then press **F6** (Bold). You will note that the entire paragraph is now bolded.

Rather than erasing and retyping paragraphs that are out of sequence or retyping sections already typed in previous pages, WordPerfect offers the option of blocking text and then moving or copying it to other locations in a document.

Move the cursor to the first letter of the beginning word in the first paragraph. Press **Alt F4** (Block) and move the cursor with the arrow keys until you have again highlighted a sentence or paragraph. Press **Ctrl F4** and you will be prompted with:

Move: 1 Block; **2** Tabular Column; **3** Rectangle: **0**

Type **1** (Block). You now see:

1 Move; **2** Copy; **3** Delete; **4** Append: **0**

Type **1** Move. You will notice that WordPerfect guides you further with the following prompt:

Move cursor; press **Enter** to retrieve.

Using the arrow keys, move the cursor beneath the second paragraph and press **Return** or **Enter**.

Move the cursor above that same paragraph, press **Return** twice, then move the cursor by pressing **Up Arrow** twice to the first of the two new blank lines. Type the following:

This paragraph will be used as an example for Blocking an entire paragraph and then deleting (erasing) it.

Move the cursor to the first letter of the beginning word in this paragraph. Press **Alt F4** (Block) and move the cursor with the arrow keys until you have highlighted the entire paragraph.

Press **Delete** or **Backspace**. WordPerfect displays:

Delete Block? (Y/N) No

Type **Y** to answer yes. You will notice that the paragraph has now been deleted.

It is possible to undelete what you just lost. Press **F1** (Cancel). WordPerfect displays:

Undelete: 1 Restore; **2 P**revious Deletion: **0**

Type **1** and your paragraph reappears.

NOTE

When undeleting, you must not press *any* other key before pressing F1 (Cancel), or the deleted material will not be recoverable.

There are several other ways to delete text in addition to blocking, backspacing, and deleting. You can delete an entire word by placing the cursor anywhere within a word and pressing **Ctrl Backspace**. Delete a line by pressing **Ctrl End** or delete several lines by pressing **Esc**, a number, and then **Ctrl End**. To delete text to the end of the page, press **Ctrl PgDn** and type **Y**.

Press **F7** (Exit), and type **N** (do not save (re-save) the document) and **N** (do not exit WP).

14

SWITCH DOCUMENT

Sometimes it is necessary to switch all uppercase text to lowercase, or vice-versa. This can be achieved by first blocking the text and then accessing WordPerfect's *Switch* feature.

EXERCISE: Switching From All Uppercase to Lowercase

Press **Caps Lock**.

Type the following:

ELEANOR ROOSEVELT ONCE SAID: "NO ONE CAN MAKE YOU FEEL INFERIOR WITHOUT YOUR CONSENT."

Press **Return**.

Press **Caps Lock** again.

Move the cursor to the first line of the paragraph at the far left margin, then press **Alt F4** (Block Options).

Press **Down Arrow** to move the block (highlight) over the entire paragraph.

Press **Shift F3** (Switch Doc.).

You will be prompted with:

   1 Uppercase; **2** Lowercase: **0**

Type **2** (Lowercase).

As you can see, the entire paragraph has now been converted to lowercase.

In the office, it is not uncommon to be interrupted in the middle of typing a document and asked to get out a "rush" instead. Rather than save and exit the present document and begin another, WordPerfect has a *Switch Doc.* feature that allows the user to move back and forth between two different documents with just a couple of keystrokes.

EXERCISE: Screen Switch

With the upper/lowercase paragraph still on the screen, press **Shift F3** (Switch Doc.).   *? 2nd*

Looking at the WordPerfect display line, you will notice that this screen is called Doc. 2.

Type the following:

Dear Jan:

    My boss is driving me crazy today —

Now pretend for a moment that your boss is walking towards you.

Press **Shift F3** (Switch Doc.).

Now your upper/lowercase document is back on screen while your personal letter is hidden safely away from curious onlookers.

Switch Doc. is also handy for those rush job interruptions that normally cause time-consuming beginnings and endings from one project to another. Instead of exiting and saving one document to begin another, Switch Doc. lets you switch back and forth interchangeably.

Another Switch Doc. shortcut is using the two screens to block/copy information from one screen/document to another.

EXERCISE: Block/Copying and Working Interchangeably Between Screens

Press **Shift F3** (Switch Doc.).

With the arrow keys, move the cursor to the first line of the letter.

Press **Alt F4** (Block). Move the cursor through the letter until all of the words are highlighted.

Press **Ctrl F4** (Move).

Type **1** (Block).

Type **2** (Copy).

Press **Shift F3** (Switch Doc.).

With the arrow keys, move the cursor to the bottom of the page with Eleanor Roosevelt's quote.

Press **Return** and the letter is copied under Eleanor Roosevelt's quote.

Being able to move/copy back and forth between screens is a timesaver since it becomes unnecessary to exit and save out of one document to go into another, then back again.

EXERCISE: Exiting Both Screens

Press **Shift F3** (Switch Doc.).

Press **F7** (Exit). You will be prompted with:

Save document? (Y/N) Yes

Type **N**. Then you are prompted with:

Exit doc. 2? (Y/N) No

Type **Y**.

Press **F7** (Exit) again. You will then be prompted with:

Save document? (Y/N) Yes

Type **N**. Then you are prompted with:

Exit WP? (Y/N) No

Type **N**.

Press **Shift F3** (Switch Doc.) twice, first into Doc 2 and back again to Doc 1.

Doc 1 and Doc 2 should be clear and the cursor should be at the top of the WordPerfect starting screen, Doc 1.

15

FOOTNOTES AND ENDNOTES

Research papers and other academic documents often require the insertion of *footnotes* and *endnotes*. In the days of standard typewriters, it was necessary to count the number of lines on a page, being sure to leave room for the footnotes and making necessary line spacing changes, and repaginate if text was added or deleted.

WordPerfect has simplified all of that and created a simple footnote and endnote format.

EXERCISE: Creating a Footnote

Press **F5** (List Files) and retrieve **your-doc.ltr**.

Using the arrow keys, move the cursor to the end of the word "ambivalence" and press **Ctrl F7** (Footnote). WordPerfect displays the following:

> **1** Footnote; **2** Endnote; **3** Endnote Placement: **0**

Type **1** (Footnote). WordPerfect then shows:

> **Footnote: 1** Create; **2** Edit; **3** New Number;
> **4** Options: **0**

Type **1** to create a footnote. The following screen will appear:

```
  1
```

Press Exit when done   Doc 1 Pg 1 Ln 2.5" Pos 1.55"

Ctrl F7 - Footnote Creation Screen

Please note that your footnote number has been inserted for you.

Type **World Poetry, 1983**

Please look over the screen. As prompted, press **F7** (Exit) when done.

NOTE

The number will not appear as a superscript or subscript on the screen. Depending on the printer you are using, the number may or may not print as a superscript or subscript, even though it is programmed to do so. Certain printers (some dot matrix, for example) may not have the capability of printing half-up lines.

Endnotes

Endnotes are listed at the end of a document, on the last page, whereas footnotes fall at the bottom of each footnoted page. To create endnotes, follow the same procedure as outlined in the previous steps, except choose **2** (Endnotes) from the **Ctrl F7** (Footnotes) menu.

16

VIEW DOCUMENT

You may like a preview of what the document will look like once printed on paper. WordPerfect offers the opportunity to *View* the document in formatted form.

EXERCISE: Viewing a Document

Press **Shift F7** to access the following Print menu:

```
Print

        1 - Full Document
        2 - Page
        3 - Document on Disk
        4 - Control Printer
        5 - Type Through
        6 - View Document
        7 - Initialize Printer

Options

        S - Select Printer            Star NX-1000
        B - Binding                   0"
        N - Number of Copies          1
        G - Graphics Quality          Medium
        T - Text Quality              High




    Selection: 0
```

Shift F7 - Print Format Menu

Type **6** (View Document).

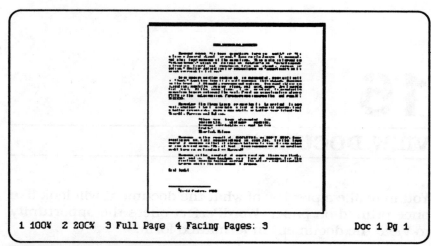

1 100% 2 20C% 3 Full Page 4 Facing Pages: 3   Doc 1 Pg 1

Shift F7; 6 - View Document screen

This display shows how WordPerfect has inserted the footnote at the bottom of the page.

View Document Menu Choices

At the bottom of the View Document screen, WordPerfect displays the choices 100%, 200%, Full Page, and Facing Pages.

Select *100%* and *200%* to bring the text closer and larger.

Select *Full Page* to view the entire page.

Select *Facing Pages* to view both the preceding page and the current page, side-by-side.

When finished, press **F1** (Cancel) several times until the menus are cleared from the screen and text is restored.

To print what you see on the screen, press **Shift Print Screen**. What is on your screen at this time should now be printing so that you may examine the footnote just completed.

NOTE

Shift Print Screen only prints the text that is seen on the screen at this time. It is also important to know that Shift Print Screen does not work on all WordPerfect supported printers.

Press **F7** (Exit), and type **N** (do not save) and **N** (do not exit WP).

17

SORTING BY ALPHABETICAL ORDER/MERGING DOCUMENTS

Lengthy lists of names, addresses, or various other information can easily be sorted and placed in alphabetical order by using WordPerfect's *Sort* feature.

Sort can be used to rearrange words, lines, paragraphs, and merge records. This will alleviate the need for extensive editing and reorganization by hand.

EXERCISE: Sorting Alphabetically, Last Name First

Type the following list of names:

Carr, Sheila
Jacobs, Anthony
Lambert, John
Hertzen, Lydia
Smith, Dave
Williams, Rhonda
Winston, Aleia
Delaney, Shelley
Karr, Katrina
Grey, Dean
Kelper, Colin
Brown, Avery
Orton, Missy
Jones, Renee
Barton, Steve
Taylor, Travis
Franklin, Wanda

> **Lancing, Janice**
> **Henning, Autumn**
> **Morgan, Melody**
> **Varnell, Elaine**
> **Smith, Lois**
> **Lewis, Jo Anne**
> **McCullock, Drew**
> **Rogers, Jeanie**

Press **Ctrl F9** (Merge/Sort). WordPerfect displays the following screen:

```
Jacobs, Anthony
Lambert, John
Hertzen, Lydia
Smith, Dave
Williams, Rhonda
Winston, Aleia
Delaney, Shelley
Karr, Katrina
Grey, Dean
Kelper, Colin
Brown, Avery
Orton, Missy
Jones, Renee
Barton, Steve
Taylor, Travis
Franklin, Wanda
Lancing, Janice
Henning, Autumn
Morgan, Melody
Varnell, Elaine
Smith, Lois
Lewis, Jo Anne
McCullock, Drew
Rogers, Jeanie
1 Merge: 2 Sort: 3 Sort Order: 0
```

Ctrl F9 - Merge/Sort Menu

Type **2** (Sort).

You will see:

Input file to sort: (Screen)

Press **Return**.   *ie. Enter*

Output file for sort: (Screen)

Press **Return**.   *ie. Enter*

The following menu appears:

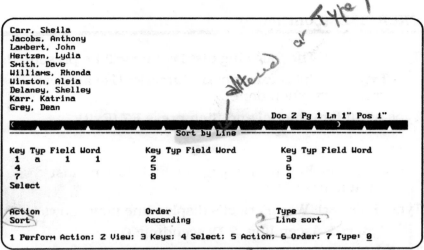

```
Carr, Sheila
Jacobs, Anthony
Lambert, John
Hertzen, Lydia
Smith, Dave
Williams, Rhonda
Winston, Aleia
Delaney, Shelley
Karr, Katrina
Grey, Dean
                                          Doc 2 Pg 1 Ln 1" Pos 1"
(                                                             )
━━━━━━━━━━━━━━━━━━━━━ Sort by Line ━━━━━━━━━━━━━━━━━━━━━━━

Key Typ Field Word        Key Typ Field Word        Key Typ Field Word
 1   a    1    1           2                         3
 4                         5                         6
 7                         8                         9
Select


Action                    Order                     Type
Sort                      Ascending                 Line sort

1 Perform Action: 2 View: 3 Keys: 4 Select: 5 Action: 6 Order: 7 Type: 0
```

Ctrl F9 Merge/Sort; 2 - Sort Action Menu *GO TO HELP*

Sort Menu Options

The Sort menu displays the following options at the bottom of the screen:

1 Perform Actions Begins the sort.

2 View Enables the user to scroll through the document.

3 Keys Specifies which word should be sorted, either by last name first (Key 1) or by first name first (Key 2). *See HELP*

> **Typ** indicates if Keys are alphanumeric (letters and numbers) or numeric only.

4 Select Sorts records that meet specific conditions (such as records with a particular zip code).

5 Action Specifies whether to select *and* sort, or just to select.

6 Order Enables the user to specify whether the sort will be performed in ascending order (from A to Z) or descending order (from Z to A).

7 Type Specifies which type of sort is desired: merge, line, or paragraph.

Use column for address list
+ 7!

63

EXERCISE: (Continued)

Type **3** (Keys). The following display line will be presented:

Type: **a**=Alphanumeric; **n**=Numeric; Use arrows; Press **Exit** when done

Type **a** (Alphanumeric) and then press **F7** (Exit).

NOTE

Default Key position is set at 1 to sort last name first.

Type **6** (Order). WordPerfect's display line now shows:

Order: 1 Ascending; **2** Descending: **0**

Type **1** (Ascending).

Type **7** (Type). WordPerfect's display line prompts with:

Type: 1 Merge; **2** Line; **3** Paragraph; **0**

Type **2** (Line).

Type **1** (Perform Action).

WordPerfect's display line will show a number of records being transferred. The Sort procedure will end with each last name in alphabetical order.

```
Barton, Steve
Brown, Avery
Carr, Sheila
Delaney, Shelley
Franklin, Wanda
Grey, Dean
Henning, Autumn
Hertzen, Lydia
Jacobs, Anthony
Jones, Renee
Karr, Katrina
Kelper, Colin
Lambert, John
Lancing, Janice
Lewis, Jo Anne
McCullock, Drew
Morgan, Melody
Orton, Missy
Rogers, Jeanie
Smith, Dave
Smith, Lois
Taylor, Travis
Varnell, Elaine
Williams, Rhonda
                              Doc 1 Pg 1 Ln 1" Pos 1"
```

To clear the screen press **F7** (Exit) and type **N** (do not save) and **N** (do not exit WP).

Merging Files

WordPerfect offers a process by which text from two different files can be combined to create letters, address lists and forms, etc. This process is called *merging*.

WordPerfect utilizes the *Merge* feature by using a primary and secondary file. The *primary* file contains text (usually a letter of correspondence) which will be repeated frequently because of numerous addressees. The *secondary* file contains the information, such as the names and addresses, which will be inserted into the primary file letter.

EXERCISE: Creating Primary and Secondary Files/Merge Codes

Type the following Primary file letter:

Center and insert the date by pressing **Shift F6**, **Shift F5** and typing **2**. Then press **Return** four times.

Press **Shift F9** (Merge Codes). WordPerfect displays the following screen:

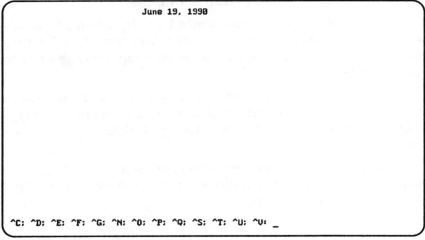

```
                    June 19, 1990
```

```
^C: ^D: ^E: ^F: ^G: ^N: ^O: ^P: ^Q: ^S: ^T: ^U: ^V: _
```

Shift F9 - Merge Codes Menu

Type **F**. Beside the Field: prompt type **1** and press **Return** twice.

The Field 1 code now appears for the first addressee line.

Press **Shift F9** (Merge Codes). Type **F**. Beside Field: type **2** and press **Return** twice.

The Field 2 code now appears for the title/company line.

Press **Shift F9** (Merge Codes). Type **F**. Beside Field: type **3** and press **Return** twice.

The Field 3 code now appears for the street address.

Press **Shift F9** (Merge Codes). Type **F**. Beside Field: type **4** and press **Return** three times.

The Field 4 code now appears for the city/state/zip.

Type **Dear**, press the **Spacebar**, and press **Shift F9** (Merge Codes). Type **F**. Beside Field: type **5** and press **Return** three times.

Continue typing the following text:

You are cordially invited to attend an art showing at Chase-Harding Gallery on Thursday, October 23rd at 7:00 p.m. Featured will be the works of Storme Erlington entitled:

Various Shades of Jade

Storme's work has captivated art lovers and critics alike, beckoning the eyes to enter her world of texture and complexity, exotic to the outer edges and woven in night moods.

Various Shades of Jade conveys a depth of discipline exceeding the normal confines of standard artistry. Light abounds, but the pervading darkness ignites to radiance.

Be our guest and experience Storme's talented works. Appetizers and cocktails will be served in the Silk Room following the showing.

Caroline Chase-Harding

The beginning of the completed letter should look like the
following illustration:

```
 —                        June 19, 1990



^F1^
^F2^
^F3^
^F4^

Dear ^F5^

      You are cordially invited to attend an art showing at Chase-
Harding Gallery on Thursday, October 23rd at 7:00 p.m. Featured
will be the works of Storme Erlington entitled:

                      Various Shades of Jade

      Storme's work has captivated art lovers and critics alike,
beckoning the eyes to enter her world of texture and complexity,
exotic to the outer edges and woven in night moods.

      Various Shades of Jade conveys a depth of discipline
exceeding the normal confines of standard artistry. Light
abounds, but the pervading darkness ignites to radiance.

                                    Doc 1 Pg 1 Ln 1" Pos 1"
```

Shell letter as it appears with Merge Codes/Fields

Press **F7** (Exit), type **Y**, save as **a:primary.ltr**, then type **N**
(do not exit WP).

Type the following address list which will be merged as a
secondary file with the primary file letter:

James E. Jones	press **F9** (Merge Field)
Jones Corporation	press **F9** (Merge Field)
333 Sunny Lane, Suite 4	press **F9** (Merge Field)
Santa Monica, CA	press **F9** (Merge Field)
Mr. Jones:	press **F9** (Merge Field)

Press **Ctrl E** to end this merge file, and press **Return** twice.

Lydia G. Smythe	press **F9** (Merge Field)
Smythe Consulting	press **F9** (Merge Field)
1707 Mockingbird Court	press **F9** (Merge Field)
Brentwood, CA	press **F9** (Merge Field)
Ms. Smythe:	press **F9** (Merge Field)

Press **Ctrl E** to end this merge file, and press **Return** twice.

Tom and Leigh Garver	press **F9** (Merge Field)
Art Consultants	press **F9** (Merge Field)
4015 Sandpiper Rock	press **F9** (Merge Field)
Malibu, CA	press **F9** (Merge Field)
Tom and Leigh:	press **F9** (Merge Field)

Press **Ctrl E** to end this merge file, and press **Return** twice.

Ted Foxworthe	press **F9** (Merge Field)
Brush Works, Ltd.	press **F9** (Merge Field)
2990 Ocean Blue Drive	press **F9** (Merge Field)
Marina del Rey, CA	press **F9** (Merge Field)
Mr. Foxworthe:	press **F9** (Merge Field)

Press **Ctrl E** to end this merge file, and press **Return** twice.

Melody Perkins	press **F9** (Merge Field)
The Tinted Tree	press **F9** (Merge Field)
9865 Gull Pointe	press **F9** (Merge Field)
Santa Monica, CA	press **F9** (Merge Field)
Melody:	press **F9** (Merge Field)

Press **Ctrl E** to end this merge file, and press **Return** twice.

Press **Pg Up** and your screen should now look like:

```
James E. Jones^R
Jones Corporation^R
333 Sunny Lane, Suite 4^R
Santa Monica, CA^R
Mr. Jones:^R
^E

Lydia G. Smythe^R
Smythe Consulting^R
1707 Mockingbird Court^R
Brentwood, CA^R
Ms. Smythe^R
^E

Tom and Leigh Garver^R
Art Consultants^R
4015 Sandpiper Rock^R
Malibu, CA^R
Tom and Leigh:^R
^E

Ted Foxworthe^R
Brush Works, Ltd.^R
2990 Ocean Blue Drive^R
                                        Doc 1 Pg 1 Ln 1" Pos 1"
```

Secondary File Merge List

Press **F7** (Exit), type **Y**, save as **a:Secondry.ltr**, then type **N** (do not exit WP).

The primary file has been created and saved, as well as the secondary file. It is now time to merge both documents into a completed letter format.

EXERCISE: Merging Primary and Secondary Files

Press **Ctrl F9** (Merge/Sort).

Type **1** (Merge).

You will be prompted with:

Primary File:

Type **Primary.ltr** and press **Return**.

You will be prompted with:

Secondary File:

Type **Secondry.ltr** and press **Return**.

Merging will appear at the bottom left corner of the screen. When WordPerfect has completed the merge, the finished letters will appear on screen, divided by hard page breaks which were automatically inserted during the merging process.

Press **Home, Home, Up Arrow** to go to the first page of your merged document. The screen appears as follows:

```
  _                     June 19, 1990


James E. Jones
Jones Corporation
333 Sunny Lane, Suite 4
Santa Monica, CA
Dear Mr. Jones:

     You are cordially invited to attend an art showing at Chase-
Harding Gallery on Thursday, October 23rd at 7:00 p.m. Featured
will be the works of Storme Erlington entitled:

                    Various Shades of Jade

     Storme's work has captivated art lovers and critics alike,
beckoning the eyes to enter her world of texture and complexity,
exotic to the outer edges and woven in night moods.

     Various Shades of Jade conveys a depth of discipline
exceeding the normal confines of standard artistry. Light
abounds, but the pervading darkness ignites to radiance.

                              Doc 1 Pg 1 Ln 1" Pos 1"
```

Press **F7** (Exit), and type **N** (do not save) and **N** (do not exit WP).

18

TEXT / COLUMNS

WordPerfect offers two distinct types of columns which are generally used for the continuous flow of text from one column to another:

Newspaper (words flow continuously down and up columns across a page); and

Parallel (used for scripts or lists).

WordPerfect also provides *Parallel with Block Protect*. This feature ensures that the text is protected from being split by a page break. If one column is extended past the page, WordPerfect's block protect adjusts that block of text to the next page.

EXERCISE: Creating Columns

An employee address list is a good example for the use of parallel columns:

Press **Alt F7** (Math/Columns). You will see the following display prompt:

1 Math On; **2** Math Def; **3** Column On/Off; **4** Column **Def: 0**

Type **4** (Column Def).

WordPerfect displays the following screen:

```
Text Column Definition

    1 - Type                            Newspaper

    2 - Number of Columns               2

    3 - Distance Between Columns

    4 - Margins

    Column    Left      Right     Column    Left      Right
      1:      1"        4"          13:
      2:      4.5"      7.5"        14:
      3:                            15:
      4:                            16:
      5:                            17:
      6:                            18:
      7:                            19:
      8:                            20:
      9:                            21:
     10:                            22:
     11:                            23:
     12:                            24:

Selection: 0
```

Alt F7 - Math/Columns Text Column Definition Menu

Type **1** (Type) then type **3** (Parallel with Block Protect).

Type **2** (Number of Columns) and press **Return**.

Type **3** (Distance Between Columns).

Press **Return** to accept the default (0.5").

Press **F7** to display the Math/Column menu.

Type **3** (Column On/Off) to turn the columns on.

Address List for Columns

Type the following addressees as listed below.

James E. Jones
333 Sun Lane
Santa Monica, CA

Lydia G. Smythe
1707 Mockingbird
Brentwood, CA

Tom and Leigh Garr
4015 Sandpiper Lane
Malibu, CA

Ted Farnworthe
2990 Ocean Court
Marina del Rey, CA

Melody Perkins
9865 Gull Pointe
Santa Monica, CA

Jim Wilson
325 West Palm
San Diego, CA

Rory Stephens
1350 Samuel Way
Dallas, TX

Fred Johnson
57 West 10th Place
Fort Worth, TX

Rhonda Phelps
363 Dovetail Lane
Santa Monica, CA

Jerome Washington
17750 Hudson
Dallas, TX   Press **Ctrl Enter**.

Rennie Littleton
3911 Willow Drive
Portland, OR

Ferdinand Pierce
2257 25th Street
Phoenix, AZ

Nancy Myers
2721 Marguerite
Malibu, CA

Joan Warren
4012 Stetson St.
Fort Worth, TX

Phillip Carter
3758 Sherwood Lane
Scottsdale, AZ

Drew Larsen
35 Sunnyhill Lane
Scottsdale, AZ

Sherry Bakerton
47900 Falcon Head
Portland, OR

Ruth Rothstein
6893 Jagged Cove
Malibu, CA

Merry Cox
27 Thornton Road
Hailey, VA

Mary Walling
2416 Langston Drive
St. Paul, MN

As you can see on your screen, WordPerfect has wrapped the address blocks down and up into a second column. Once the address list has been completed, editing is made easy moving column-to-column by pressing **Ctrl Home** (Go To) then **Left** or **Right Arrow**. This moves the cursor to the previous or next column using WordPerfect's **F2** (Search) feature to deliver the cursor to a desired word, name or phrase.

For practice, continue typing address blocks of your own to see how WordPerfect wraps down and up into a third column. Practice moving column-to-column by pressing **Ctrl Home, Down Arrow,** and using the **F2** (Search) options.

Press **F7** (Exit), and type **N** (do not save) and **N** (do not exit WP).

19

ADVANCED EDITING/SEARCH FORWARD/SEARCH REVERSE/ GLOBAL SEARCH AND REPLACE

As stated previously, WordPerfect has superior editing features that can cut revision time in half, making the tedious job of editing faster and more productive. One such editing feature is the *Search* option. Rather than proceed through a page line-by-line, you can search forward or backward through a document to a particular word or phrase.

Additionally, WordPerfect's Search/Replace performs *globally* (throughout the file), searching through a document and pausing at the desired word/phrase and prompting for the replacement of a new word.

It is also possible to search for a page by page number. This is achieved by pressing **Ctrl Home** (7 on the 10-key pad), typing the page number, then pressing **Return**. The cursor moves directly from the previous position to the top of the specified page.

The following exercise guides you through the search features. Please notice how quickly the cursor moves to the searched word or phrase and how much editing time can be saved by utilizing these features.

EXERCISE: Accessing Search Features

→ **Search**, located on the F2 key template searches forward in a document to a particular word, phrase, or command and stops the cursor there.

Press **F5** (List Files) and retrieve **your-doc.ltr**.

Press **Pg Up** (9 on the 10-key pad) to move to the top of the page.

Press **F2**. You will be prompted with:

    → **Srch:**

Type **fruit** and then press **Esc**. WordPerfect moves the cursor to the word "fruit."

To search backward, press **Shift F2** (← Search), type **ambivalence** and press **Esc** to instruct the computer to look for "ambivalence." Notice that the cursor moved backward through the document to the word "ambivalence."

It will sometimes be necessary to globally replace a name or particular word or phrase within a document.

Press **Pg Up** to move the cursor to the beginning of your-doc.

Press **Alt F2** (Replace). You will be prompted with:

    w/Confirm? (Y/N) No

This question means: Do you prefer that the cursor stop at each name, word, or phrase and allow you to confirm that you would like to replace it with the new word/phrase?

NOTE

It is a good idea to say "yes" here because sometimes a word can be found within another word. Example: "and" inside the word "hand."

Type **Y** to select yes, confirm. You will then be prompted with:

    → **Srch:**

Type the word **dreams** and press **Esc.** ,

WordPerfect then displays the following prompt:

Replace with:

Type the word **wishes** and press **Esc**.

At this time the cursor stops at the word "dreams" and prompts you with **Confirm? (Y/N)**. To replace the word type **Y** for yes. Once the Search/Replace is finished, WordPerfect no longer displays the **Confirm? (Y/N)** prompt.

Press **Pg Up** (9 on the 10-key pad).

20

SETTING FORMATS

Sometimes it is necessary to change *line format* settings for line spacing, margins, tabs, and various other formats within a document. You may also utilize *page formatting* features for automatically numbering pages and to create headers and footers (a single phrase that repetitively prints at the top (head) or bottom (foot) of given pages.)

EXERCISE: Accessing Shift F8 (Format) Menu

Press **Shift F8** (Format). You will see the following:

```
Format

    1 - Line
              Hyphenation                     Line Spacing
              Justification                   Margins Left/Right
              Line Height                     Tab Set
              Line Numbering                  Widow/Orphan Protection

    2 - Page
              Center Page (top to bottom)     New Page Number
              Force Odd/Even Page             Page Numbering
              Headers and Footers             Paper Size/Type
              Margins Top/Bottom              Suppress

    3 - Document
              Display Pitch                   Redline Method
              Initial Codes/Font              Summary

    4 - Other
              Advance                         Overstrike
              Conditional End of Page         Printer Functions
              Decimal Characters              Underline Spaces/Tabs
              Language

Selection: 0
```

Shift F8 - Format Menu

For basic WordPerfect applications, 1 (Line) and 2 (Page) format sections will be covered in this section.

Type **1** (Line). The following menu is displayed:

```
Format: Line

    1 - Hyphenation                      Off

    2 - Hyphenation Zone - Left          10%
                          Right          4%

    3 - Justification                    Yes

    4 - Line Height                      Auto

    5 - Line Numbering                   No

    6 - Line Spacing                     1

    7 - Margins - Left                   1"
                  Right                  1"

    8 - Tab Set                          0", every 0.5"

    9 - Widow/Orphan Protection          No


Selection: 0
```

Shift F8 - Line Format Menu

Hyphenation means that the computer will make decisions on whether or not a word needs to be hyphenated.

Type **1** (Hyphenation). You are prompted with:

1 Off; 2 Manual; 3 Auto: 0

If you preferred hyphenation to be off, then you would select 1. If you would like hyphenation to be on and for the computer to pause at each hyphenation occurrence and beep, then you would select 2. If you would like hyphenation to be performed automatically without pausing and beeping, you would select 3. For our exercises, type **1** to turn hyphenation <u>off</u>.

Justification means that the right margin of the document is always straight, like in a newspaper column. Some people like the look of this. Others prefer the traditional typing style of an uneven right margin, as justification can sometimes leave too many unattractive gaps between words.

Type **3** (Justification). You will be prompted with a blinking cursor under **Yes**. If you would prefer to turn justification off, type **N** for No.

Line Spacing is available in single spacing, one and a half, double, or triple spacing.

Type **6** (Line Spacing). You will be prompted with a blinking cursor under the 1. For our exercise, leave the spacing at 1 and press **Return**. It is helpful to remember that the text you are working on is still on the screen beneath this menu and a line spacing change would reformat the document automatically.

Margins are set at a default of 1" on each side. Normally, you will not need to change the margins, but if you do, it is quite simple.

Type **7** (Margins - Left/Right). You will be prompted with a blinking cursor under the 1. Type a new number here to increase or decrease the left margin and repeat the number change for the right margin. To complete the change press **Return**. The margin change affects text from that point on.

Tabs are automatically set in increments of five spaces. Tab settings can be changed at any point in a document. The tabs are presented on a ruler at the bottom of the screen with "L's" indicating each individual tab.

Type **8** (Tab Set).

You will be prompted with the following menu:

```
                        THE SECRET OF SUCCESS


            Succeed means "to have something turn out well." or "to
   attain a desired object or end." Some people desire to succeed,
   yet also fear success at the same time. This state is termed as
   "ambivalence." which is defined in Webster's as "simultaneous
   attraction toward and repulsion from an object, person or
   action." Another definition for ambivalence is "uncertainty as to
   which approach to follow."

            Upon seeing another person who is successful, many will
   call it "luck." Luck has less to do with success than effort.
   Success is the fruit of thought. purpose and action. One must
   obtain an objective, mentally draw up plans, and work every day
   towards that goal. At the same time, it is important to
   constantly visualize having achieved the goal. Positive
   visualization stamps FAITH on the subconscious. Perseverance
   assures the end result: SUCCESS.

   L....L....L....L....L....L....L....L....L....L....L....L....L....L....
   T    ^    !    ^    !    ^    !    ^    !    ^    !    ^    !    ^    !    ^
   1"        2"        3"        4"        5"        6"        7"        8"
   Delete EOL (clear tabs): Enter Number (set tab): Del (clear tab):
   Left: Center: Right: Decimal: .= Dot Leader
```

Shift F8; 1 - Line Format Tab Menu

Delete EOL means to press the key combination which enables you to delete an entire line of text. To clear the tabs, press **Ctrl End**. Notice that all the "L's" are now deleted.

To set your own tabs type a number at the prompt and press **Return**. For instance, to insert a tab at 15, type **1.5** and press **Return**. A tab "L" has now been inserted on the tab line.

To accept the tab setting changes, you would press F7 (Exit) to insert the new settings into the document. Since you do not need to actually change the tabs in your present document, press **F1** to cancel out of the tab setting menu.

Widow/Orphan is a "straggling line" at the bottom or top of a page. Rather than have a paragraph break with a single line at either the top or bottom of the page, WordPerfect offers the option to protect paragraphs from single-line breaks.

To allow **Widow/Orphan** protection type **9** from the Format menu.

Type **Y** for yes.

Press **F7** (Exit) to return to the text on screen.

To continue in format instruction, press **Shift F8** (Format) again.

Type **2** (Page) Format.

You will now see the following menu:

```
Format: Page

    1 - Center Page (top to bottom)     No

    2 - Force Odd/Even Page

    3 - Headers

    4 - Footers

    5 - Margins - Top                   1"
                  Bottom                1"

    6 - New Page Number                 1
          (example: 3 or iii)

    7 - Page Numbering                  No page numbering

    8 - Paper Size                      8.5" x 11"
           Type                         Standard

    9 - Suppress (this page only)

Selection: 0
```

Shift F8; 2 - Page Format Menu

Center Page is used in journalism and sometimes for heading pages. If you would like to have an entire page of text centered, then type 1 to change it to Yes. At this time, however, leave it at "No."

Headers and **Footers** are used to list a title, name, or phrase at the top of every page as a *header*, or at the bottom of every page as a *footer*.

Type **3** (Header). You will be prompted with:

1 Header **A**; **2** Header **B**: **0**

Type **1** (Header A). You will then see the following menu:

1 Discontinue; 2 Every Page; 3 Odd Pages; **4** Even Pages; **5 Edit**: **0**

Type **2** (Every Page).

Type the following:

Winning in Life
Page (now press **Ctrl B**)

Your screen looks like the following:

```
Winning in Life
Page ^B_




Press Exit when done                              Ln 1.16" Pos 1.7"
```

Shift F8; 2 - Page Format Header Menu

NOTE

Ctrl B is a code which instructs the computer to consecutively number pages within a header and footer.

Press **F7** (Exit) to return to the Page Format menu.

The method for creating a footer is identical, except the footer will be printed at the bottom of every page.

Page Numbering is used to automatically number pages. Type **7** (Page Numbering). You will then see this menu:

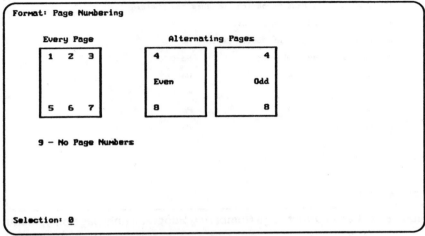

Shift F8; 2 - Page Format Page Numbering Menu

This menu shows possible positions on a page for the page number to appear. For instance, in looking at the far left rectangle, choosing "6" would instruct the computer to print a page number at the bottom center of every page.

Type **6**.

Often, it is preferred that the page number not appear on the first page of a document. In Page Format, there is a function that *suppresses* page numbering on the present page only.

NOTE

Remember to always make page format changes at the very beginning of the first page of a document.

Type **9** (Suppress this page only). You will then see:

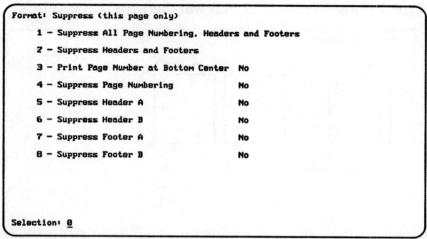

```
Format: Suppress (this page only)

    1 - Suppress All Page Numbering, Headers and Footers

    2 - Suppress Headers and Footers

    3 - Print Page Number at Bottom Center   No

    4 - Suppress Page Numbering              No

    5 - Suppress Header A                    No

    6 - Suppress Header B                    No

    7 - Suppress Footer A                    No

    8 - Suppress Footer B                    No




Selection: 0
```

Shift F8; 2 - Page Format Page Numbering Suppress (this page only) Menu

This menu allows you to suppress page numbers, headers and/or footers.

Type **4** (Suppress Page Numbering). You will be prompted with a blinking cursor under the word "No." Type **Y** for "Yes" and press **Return** three times until you are back to the document.

Press **Alt F3** (Reveal Codes) and check the codes. After looking at Reveal Codes, press **Alt F3** again to restore the screen.

Press **F7** (Exit), and type **N** (do not save the document) and **N** (do not exit WP).

21

MATH/COLUMNS AND FLUSH RIGHT

WordPerfect's *Math/Columns* feature brings light, statistical typing projects to completion in a fast and easy way. This basic math function aligns numbers at specified tabs and backs the numbers off the decimal position. No longer is it necessary to align numbers by using Backspace and Left/Right Arrows.

EXERCISE: (Math On) Tab Columns by Decimal Point

Type the following heading:

BETHANY VALLEY BI-YEARLY REPORT

Press **Return** three times.

(Tab to positions 4.5 and 6.0 to type the following subheadings:)

Spring '91   Autumn '91

Press **Return** twice.

Press **Shift F8** (Format).

Type **1** (Line Format).

Type **8** (Tab Set).

Press **Ctrl End** (on the 10-key pad) to clear tabs.

Type **5.2** and press **Return**.

Type **6.7** and press **Return**.

Press **F7** (Exit) twice.

Press **Alt F7** (Math/Columns).

Type **1** (Math On).

Continue typing the following, tabbing once to type the first number, and tabbing a second time to type the second number. (These numbers will line up neatly under the headings.)

	Spring '91	Autumn '91
Dovetail Winery	279,580.75	317,230.00
Eaglepointe Vineyards	92,430.00	98,680.00
Harvest Court	187,430.00	193,480.00
Raven Crest Winery	99,332.00	89,450.00
Shallimere Vineyards	240,165.00	249,438.00
Regency Grapes	80,072.00	79,591.00
Windy Valley Winery	133,435.00	192,380.00

Press **Return**.

Press **Alt F7** (Math Columns).

Type **1** (Math Off).

Your screen should resemble the following:

```
                    BETHANY VALLEY BI-YEARLY REPORT


                                 Spring '91      Autumn '91
         Dovetail Winery           279,580.75      317,230.00
         Eaglepointe Vineyards      92,430.00       98,680.00
         Harvest Court             187,430.00      193,480.00
         Raven Crest Winery         99,332.00       89,450.00
         Shallimere Vineyards      240,165.00      249,438.00
         Regency Grapes             80,072.00       79,591.00
         Windy Valley Winery       133,435.00      192,380.00
         _




                                              Doc 1 Pg 1 Ln 3" Pos 1"
```

Press **F7** (Exit), and type **N** (do not save) and **N** (do not exit WP).

Sometimes it may be necessary to enter text which would require a single right-hand column of numbers. By far, the most simple way to do this is by using WordPerfect's *Flush Right* feature located on the Alt F6 key. Flush Right aligns the cursor flush against the right margin. As you type, each character/number will be pushed to the left until Return (or Enter) is pressed.

EXERCISE: Flush Right

Type the following:

The following figures will reflect the competitive rates over the past fiscal year:

White Creamery, Inc.	Press **Alt F6**	**59,789.00**
Mill Valley Dell	Press **Alt F6**	**42,891.60**
Dwight Weber Farms	Press **Alt F6**	**72,590.00**
Corn Factory, Ltd.	Press **Alt F6**	**93,621.80**
Dairy-Rich, Inc.	Press **Alt F6**	**102,340.50**
Maiden Growers Co.	Press **Alt F6**	**87,331.00**
Jaime Dairy Corp.	Press **Alt F6**	**83,556.50**

Your screen should resemble the following:

```
The following figures will reflect the competitive rates over the
past fiscal year:

White Creamery, Inc.                            59,789.00
Mill Valley Dell                                42,891.60
Dwight Weber Farms                              72,590.00
Corn Factory, Ltd.                              93,621.80
Dairy-Rich, Inc.                               102,340.50
Maiden Growers Co.                              87,331.00
Jaime Dairy Corp.                               83,556.50
-




                                     Doc 1 Pg 1 Ln 2.66" Pos 1"
```

WordPerfect offers more detailed math/column applications which can be explored once basic WordPerfect skills have been established. In the meantime, these math alignment options can save time and hassle, allowing you to create perfect columns with just a few keystrokes.

Press **F7** (Exit), and type **N** (do not save) and **N** (do not exit WP).

22

MACROS

Macros are small "programs" which save every keystroke and command. Repetitive phrases such as city and state, closings on letters, page numbering format changes, or anything that will be performed redundantly should be put in a macro. The easiest way to name macros is to name them with the *Alt key* and a *letter*. The following will be an exercise for defining (creating) a macro phrase.

EXERCISE: Creating Word/Phrase Macros

Press **Ctrl F10** (Macro Define). You will be prompted with:

Define macro:

Press **Alt** and type **D**. You will then be prompted with:

Description:

Press **Return** to skip this.

You will then be prompted with:

Macro Def   {blinking}

Now type the following:

the Offices of <u>Tone and Laughter</u>, Dallas, Texas.

Press **Ctrl F10** (Macro Define). (This ends the macro exercise.)

Press **F7** (Exit), type **N** (No don't save) and type **N** (No don't exit WP) to clear the screen. Now type the following:

Please join us at

(Press **Alt D**).

Notice that by pressing **Alt D**, the phrase "the Offices of <u>Tone and Laughter</u>, Dallas, Texas." was inserted. This allows you to avoid redundant typing of this phrase in the future.

Clear the screen at this time by pressing **F7** (Exit), and typing **N** (do not save) and **N** (do not exit WP).

WordPerfect also provides an opportunity to create a macro (program) with pauses to allow the insertion of words, names, or other information at different points within the macro layout. The following exercise will exemplify a WordPerfect macro with pauses.

EXERCISE: Creating a Memorandum Macro with Pauses

Press **Ctrl F10** (Macro Define). You will be prompted with:

　　Define macro:

Press **Alt** and type **M**. You will then be prompted with:

　　Description:

Press **Return** to skip over this.

You will then be prompted with:

　　Macro Def　　{blinking}

Press **Shift F6** (Center) and type the following:

MEMORANDUM	Press **Return** three times.
TO:	Press **Tab** twice and press **Ctrl Pg Up**, type **1** (Pause), and press **Return** three times.
FROM:	Press **Tab** and **Ctrl Pg Up**, type **1** (Pause), and press **Return** three times.
DATE:	Press **Tab** and **Shift F5**, type **2** (Date Code), and press **Return** three times.
SUBJ:	Press **Tab** and **Ctrl Pg Up**, type **1** (Pause) and press **Return** three times.

Hold down **Shift Underline** and underline to the right margin at 7.5.

Press **Return** twice.

Press **Ctrl F10** (Macro Define) to end the macro definition (creation). You have now built a program that can be retrieved as needed. This program is installed with pauses (achieved by pressing the **Ctrl Pg Up** command, then **1**) after each heading to allow the typing of necessary information. Clear the screen at this time by pressing **F7** (Exit), and typing **N** (do not save) and **N** (do not exit WP).

Recalling Memorandum Macro with Pauses

To recall the memorandum macro you just created, press **Alt M.**

Notice that the cursor is situated at the first pause position after "TO:".

Type **Lynn Jones** and press **Return**.

Your cursor should now be situated at the second pause command after "FROM:".

Type **your name** and press **Return**.

As you can see, WordPerfect's Date Code was automatically inserted with today's date, and the cursor is positioned after "SUBJ:".

Type **Memorandum Macro** and press **Return**.

The cursor should now be located under the dividing line and ready for text. Your screen should resemble the following:

```
                        MEMORANDUM

TO:     Lynn Jones
FROM:   Jane Doe
DATE:   June 19, 1990
SUBJ:   Memorandum Macro
_____
-



                                    Doc 1 Pg 1 Ln 3.16" Pos 1"
```

Clear the screen at this time by pressing **F7** (Exit), and typing **N** (do not save) and **N** (do not exit WP).

You need Draw Perfect files ending with .WPG. (a Word Perfect Corporation product.)

23

GRAPHICS / CLIP-ART APPLICATION

WordPerfect 5.0 offers the option of creating *Graphics* (figures in the form of Clip-Art Images from Publisher's PicturePaks).

The following thirty images are included:

AIRPLANE.WPG

AND.WPG

ANNOUNCE.WPG

APPLAUSE.WPG

ARROW1.WPG

ARROW2.WPG

AWARD.WPG

BADNEWS.WPG

BOOK.WPG

BORDER.WPG

CHECK.WPG

CLOCK.WPG

CONFIDEN.WPG

FLAG.WPG

GAVEL.WPG

GOODNEWS.WPG

MAPSYMBL.WPG

THINKER.WPG

PC.WPG

HAND.WPG

PRESENT.WPG

USAMAP.WPG

PENCIL.WPG

HOURGLAS.WPG

QUILL.WPG

NEWSPAPR.WPG

PHONE.WPG

KEY.WPG

RPTCARD.WPG

NO1.WPG

NOTE

Please refer to the WordPerfect 5.1 Update section to see additional clip-art images available through WordPerfect 5.1.

There are several ways to access these clip-art images for creating personal stationery, announcements, or for just having fun.

EXERCISE: Creating Personal Stationery Using Clip Art

To create personal stationery:

Press **Alt F9** (Graphics). The following submenu is displayed:

1 Figure; **2** Table; **3** Text Box; **4** User-defined Box; **5** Line: **0**

Type **1** (Figure). You will then be prompted with:

Figure: 1 Create; **2** Edit; **3** New Number; **4** Options: **0**

Type **1** (Create). At this time the Graphics Figure Edit menu will appear:

```
Definition: Figure

    1 - Filename
    2 - Caption
    3 - Type                    Paragraph
    4 - Vertical Position       0"
    5 - Horizontal Position     Right
    6 - Size                    3.25" wide × 3.25" (high)
    7 - Wrap Text Around Box    Yes
    8 - Edit




Selection: 0
```

Alt F9 - Graphics Figure/Edit Menu

Type **1** (Filename) and type the full name of the clip-art image you would like to use. For example, type:

c:\book.wpg

and press **Return**.

NOTE

Graphics images may be housed in a subdirectory such as "Software" or "WP50." It will be necessary to indicate the location/directory where graphics images are housed when typing the filename. Example: C:\ SOFTWARE\BOOK.WPG

For basic "wrap around a box" stationery, you may now proceed by typing **8** (Edit). The following will appear:

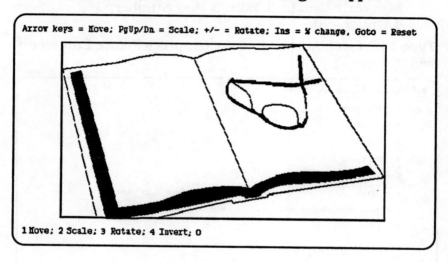

Arrow keys = Move; PgUp/Dn = Scale; +/- = Rotate; Ins = % change, Goto = Reset

1 Move; 2 Scale; 3 Rotate; 4 Invert; 0

At this time, you might want to make the clip-art image smaller. Type **2** (Scale). You will be prompted with:

Scale X: 100

To make the image half as big, type "50" instead of "100."

Repeat for Scale Y.

Press **Return** until the cursor is back to a blank page.

At the left margin, type the following text in bold and caps (remember to press **Return** after each line):

YOUR NAME
ADDRESS

CITY, STATE, ZIP
TELEPHONE

As you type, please note that the clip-art figure will be displayed as vertical lines. You will not be able to see the image itself. After typing your stationery heading, press **Return** several times and begin to type the body of your letter. Do not press **Return** as you type this time. The text will "wrap around" the box for you.

When finished, press **Shift F7** (Print) and type **6** (View the Document) so that you can see how your page will look when printed.)

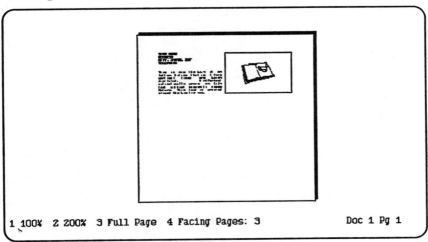

Press **F7** (Exit) to move back to the page of text.

You have now completed basic WordPerfect training. It will be beneficial to practice on letters, papers or exercises. Repetition will enable you to gain speed of application.

Good luck with your new skills!

To exit for the day, press **F7** (Exit), and type **N** (do not save) and **Y** (Yes, exit WP). Remove the disks and shut off the computer and the printer.

ADDENDUM

FORMATTING NEW DISKS

If new, previously unused work disks are being used, it will be necessary to format them so that they will be compatible with WordPerfect.

For Dual Floppy Computer Users:

Turn on the computer and load the DOS disk in drive A. Follow the date/time prompts and at the A prompt, type·

format b: and press **Return**.

The computer will instruct you to load the target disk in drive B and press Return. It will take approximately 60 seconds to format the new disk. After the disk has been formatted, write a small "f" on the label with a felt-tipped pen for future reference that the disk was formatted.

For Hard Drive Users:

Access DOS through the start-up menu selection. Repeat the procedure outlined above, except there will be no date/time prompt. Once complete, access the WordPerfect menu selection and boot as usual.

WORDPERFECT 5.1 UPDATE

WordPerfect regularly updates with new and improved features which enhance work speed and quality.

Usually, moving up an entire number (such as moving from WordPerfect 4.0/4.1/4.2 to the 5.0 series) indicates that major changes have been implemented. For example, WordPerfect introduced Graphics and a decimalized format in its 5.0 series. WordPerfect 5.1 indicates that enhancements have been made, but that basic WordPerfect features remain essentially the same.

Since WordPerfect 5.1 offers mostly basic improvements for existing methods, the following information will brief you on features that have been expanded and improved upon.

Longer Document Names

In WordPerfect 5.1, you may now name your document up to 68 characters and/or spaces. For basic WordPerfect use, however, it would be unlikely that such a long document name would be necessary. For beginner/intermediate users, it is best to keep document names concise and consistent for easy access and shorter work time.

Keyboard Layout

WordPerfect 5.1 now offers a Map Option on the Shift F1 Setup: Keyboard Layout menu. The map gives a list of keys and their functions.

Justification

For formatting pages to more precise specifications, WordPerfect 5.1 has expanded to four types of justification: text aligned on both margins; text aligned on left or right margin *only*; center justification between margins; and center or flush right multiple line alignment.

Page Numbering and Style

WordPerfect 5.1 Format Page Number menu offers the option to select Arabic, uppercase Roman, and lowercase Roman. There is also a new option for including text with the page number.

Paper Size/Type

The Page Size/Type menu has allowed more selections for pre-defined sizes of papers, forms, and envelopes.

Pull-Down Menus

The new pull-down menu feature is accessed by pressing Alt-=. To select a command, highlight the command and press Enter, or click on the command with the mouse.

Reveal Codes

The new Reveal Codes screen is adjustable. You can make it either larger or smaller while editing on screen.

Spell Check

Spell Check has been enhanced to pick up capitalization errors. (Example: THank you!)

Tabs

WordPerfect 5.1 now allows tab sets relative to the margins of choice so that the tabs will move into adjusted alignment as the margins change.

WordPerfect 5.1 Clip-art Images

The following are additional clip-art images available:

ARROW-22.WPG

BALLOONS.WPG

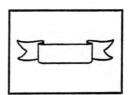

BANNER-3.WPG

BICYCLE.WPG

BKGRND-1.WPG

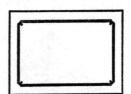

BORDER-8.WPG

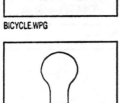

BULB.WPG

BURST-1.WPG

BUTTRFLY.WPG

CALENDAR.WPG

CERTIF.WPG

CHKBOX-1.WPG

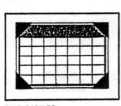

CLOCK.WPG

CNTRCT-2.WPG

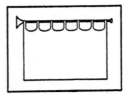

DEVICE-2.WPG

DIPLOMA.WPG

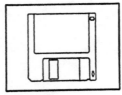

FLOPPY-2.WPG

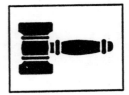

GAVEL.WPG

GLOBE2-M.WPG   HANDS-3.WPG   MAGNIF.WPG

MAILBAG.WPG   NEWS.WPG   PC-1.WPG

PRESNT-1.WPG   PRINTR-3.WPG   SCALE.WPG

STAR-5.WPG   TELPHONE.WPG   TROPHY.WPG

Index